COLORING
IS COOL

BY IBBY GREER

COLORING IS COOL

IBBY GREER

DREAMNICHE PRESS
COPYRIGHT 2015

ISBN-13: 978-1500345624
ISBN-10: 1500345628

ALL DRAWINGS AND COVER ART BY THE AUTHOR.
PAGE FRAMING AND COVER DESIGN BY
MATT MUSSELMAN
WWW.INVOKEDESIGN.US

COPIES WITH PERMISSION OF THE AUTHOR.
ETGREER@COX.NET
WWW.MOONSHINEWIDOW.COM

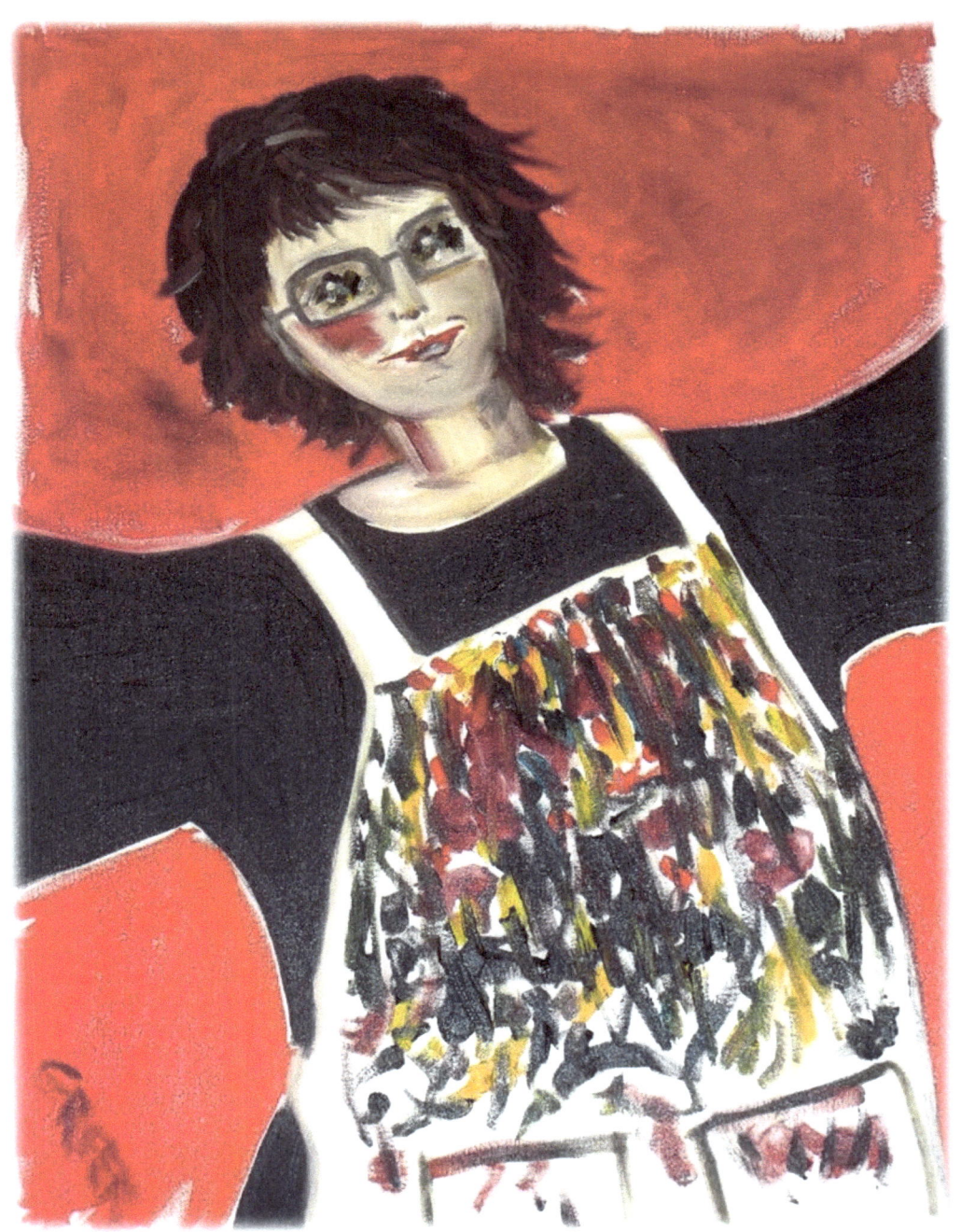

CUBES AND CORNERS, SHADOWS RACING

AROUND SHARP SQUARES

AND EMPTY WHITE SPACE.

COLOR THESE PIECES OF LENGTH, WIDTH, AND HEIGHT

WITH THE CARE YOU WOULD COLOR A FACE.

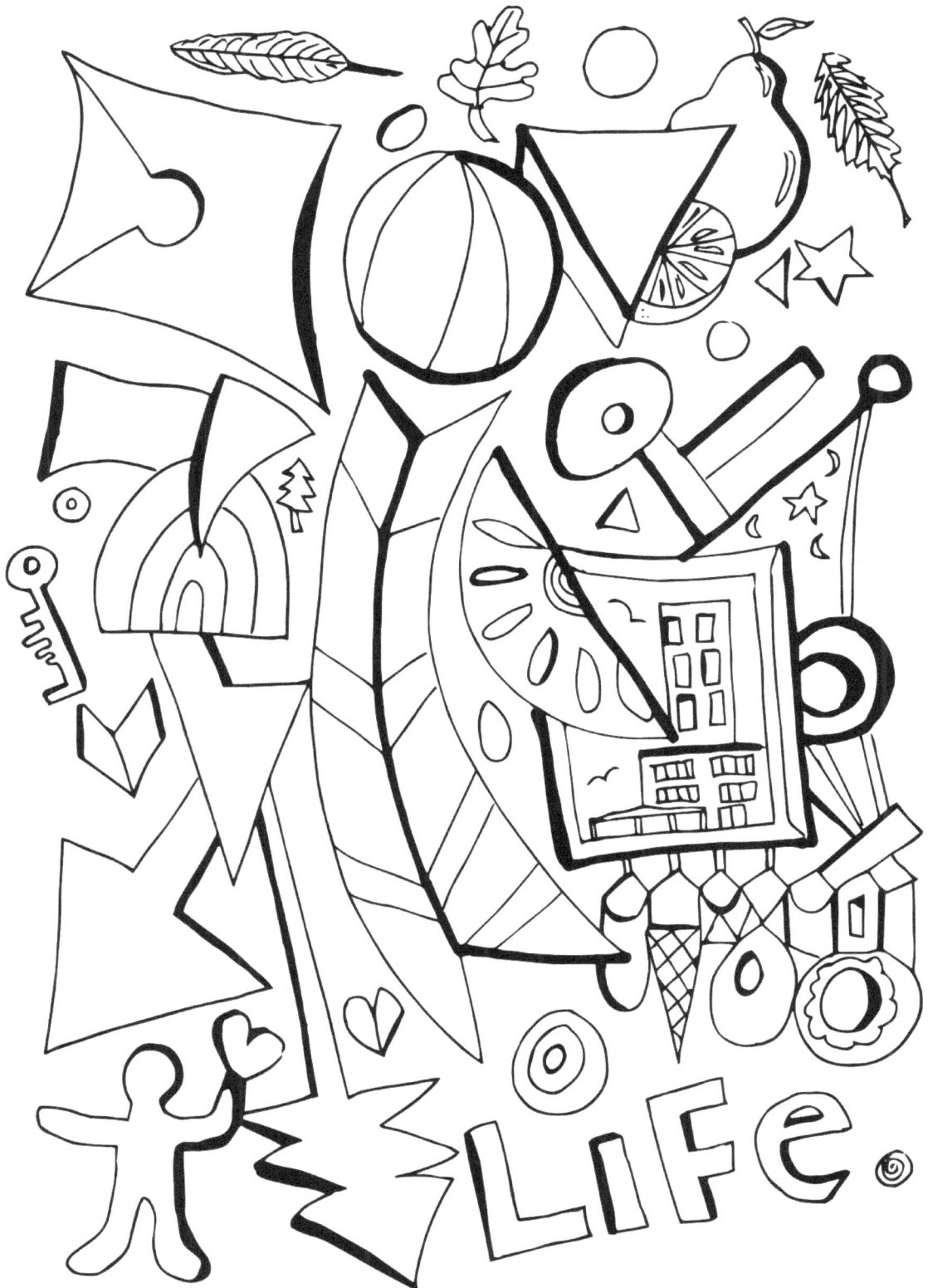

THE BEAUTIES OF NATURE
ARE AROUND US
ALL THE TIME.
SHAPES AND STARS AND
MYSTERIES!
COLOR THEM BRIGHT.

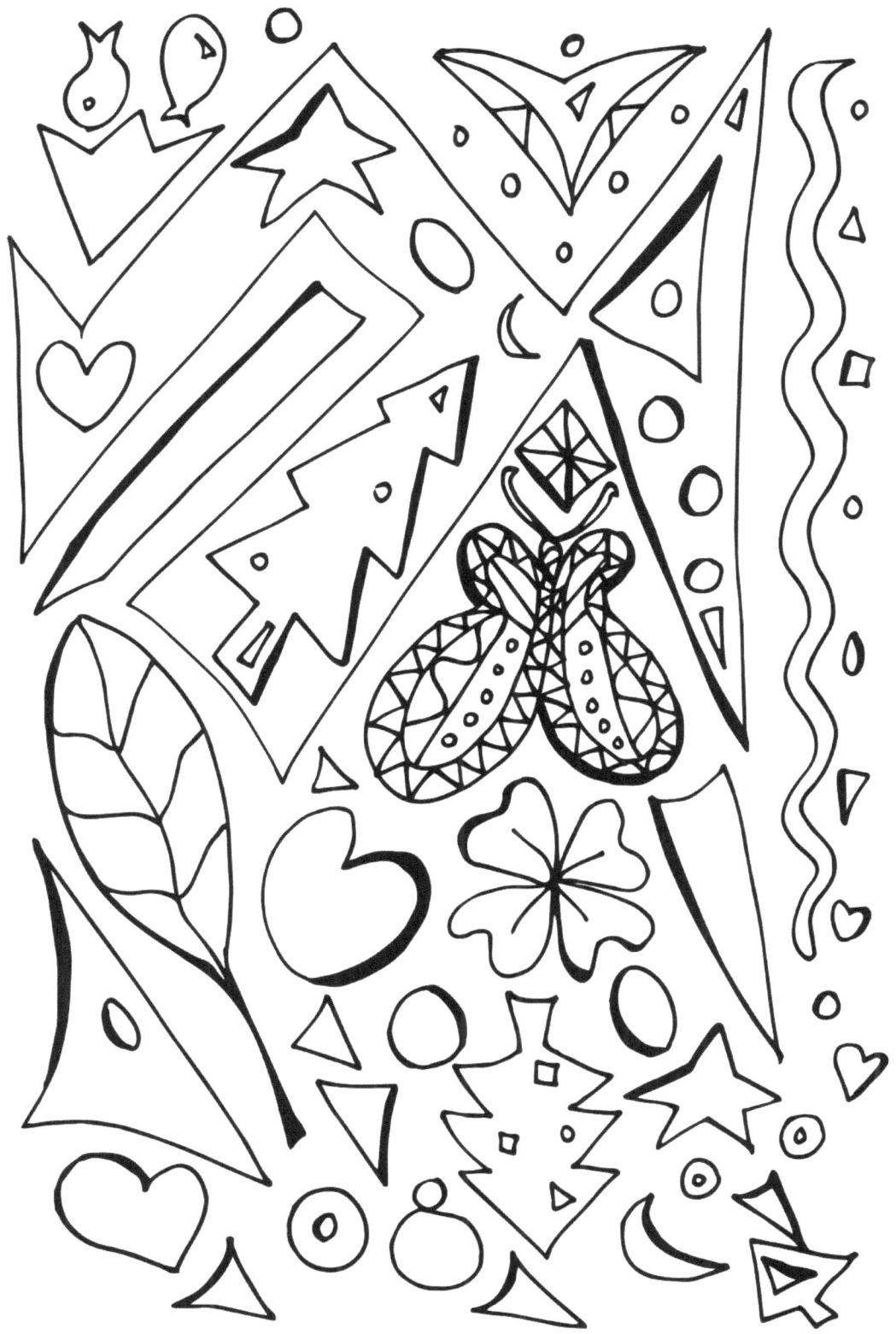

CUPS AND GLASSES, COFFEE AND WINE ?

SHERRY OR CHOCOLATE,

SERVED WHEN WE DINE ?

CUPCAKES AND CHEESE CUBES,

WEDGES OF BRIE.

COLOR THEM WELL.

THEY NOURISH ME.

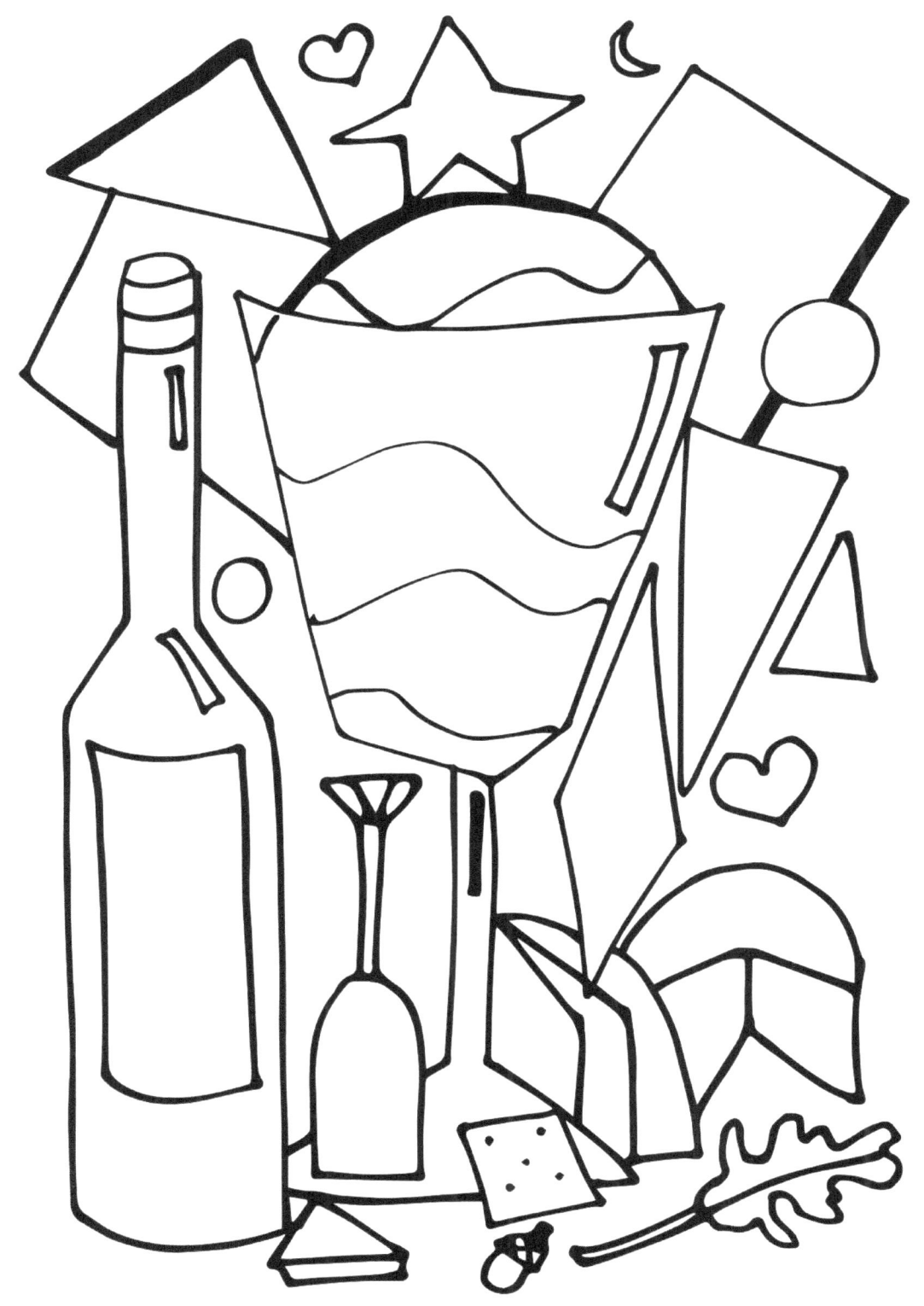

LIGHT A CANDLE.

WATCH THE CRESCENT MOON.

HOLD THE GOLD OF FIRE INSIDE

YOUR MIND AND EYE, AND SOON

THE GLOW OF LIFE

WILL NOT HIDE.

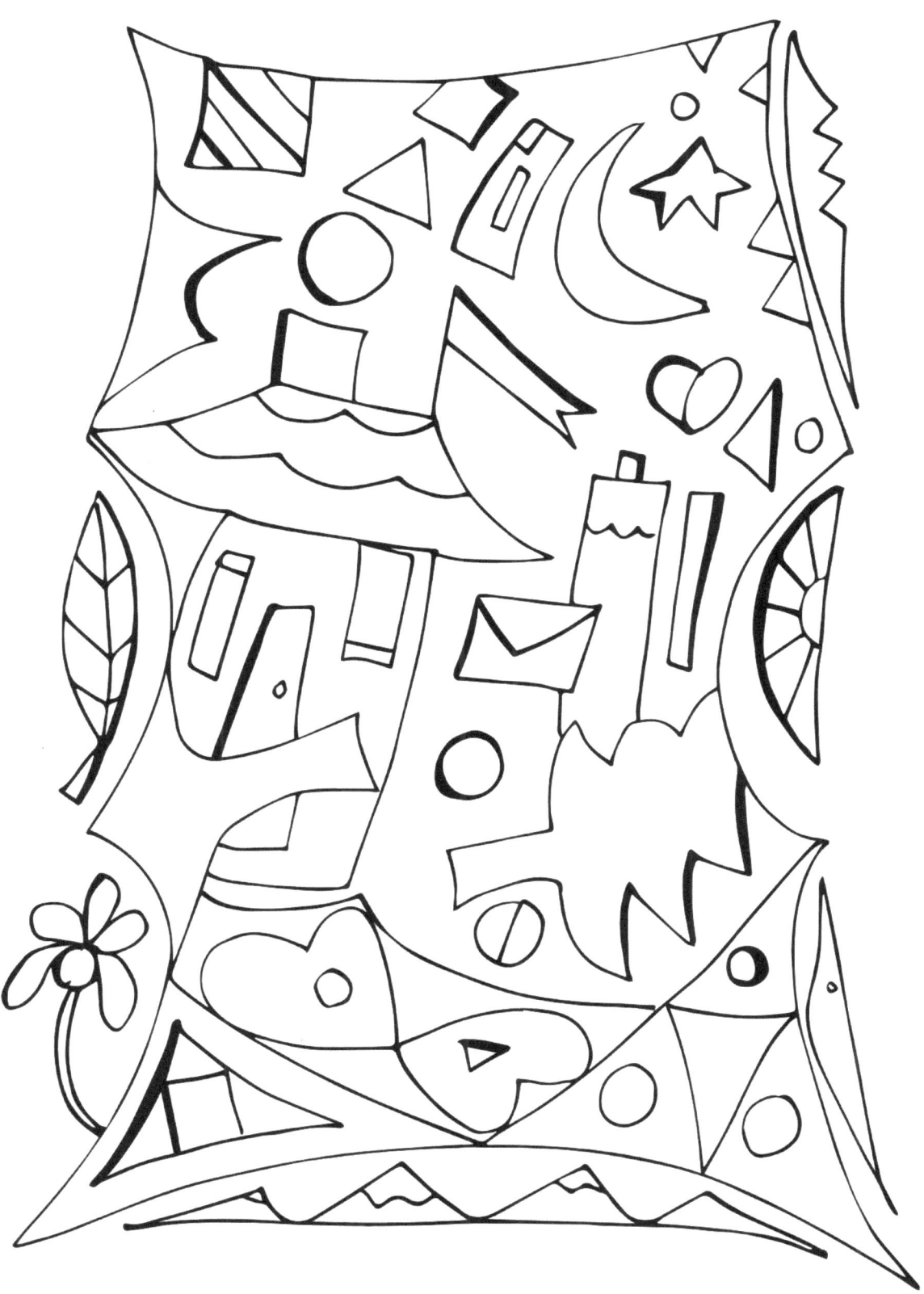

MAKE THE TIME FOR FRIENDS.

FILL YOUR LIVES WITH FUN.

MEALS AND TRIPS,

A LAUGH, A HUG,

CAMPING AND PARTYING,

WRITING LETTERS,

TAKING A CALL.

IN THE END,

WHAT WE HAVE IS,

CHOICE BY CHOICE,

LOVE, CARE, AND HOPE.

WHAT WE HAVE

IS

ALL,

ALL WE HAVE IS ALL!

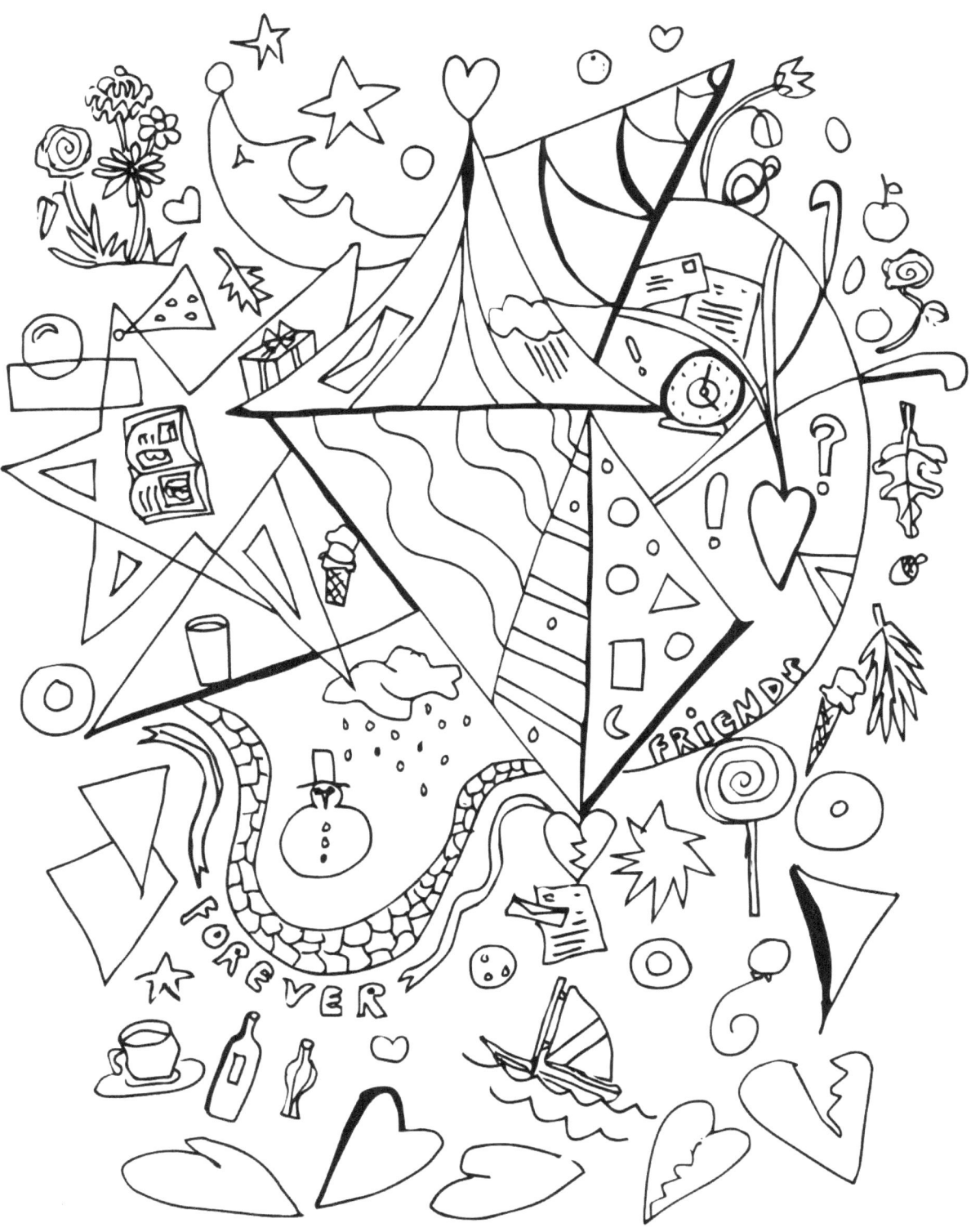

EGGS OF LIFE SO SMALL, SO GREAT,

TUCKED AMONG THE LEAVES,

WHERE BASIL BLOOMS AND ROSES BEND

AND HOUSES REST 'NEATH TREES.

STARS AND SQUARES AND CURVES AND SWIRLS

CIRCLE IN THE SKIES

AND COLORS GLOW AND COLORS FADE

WHEN YOU AND THEY ENTWINE.

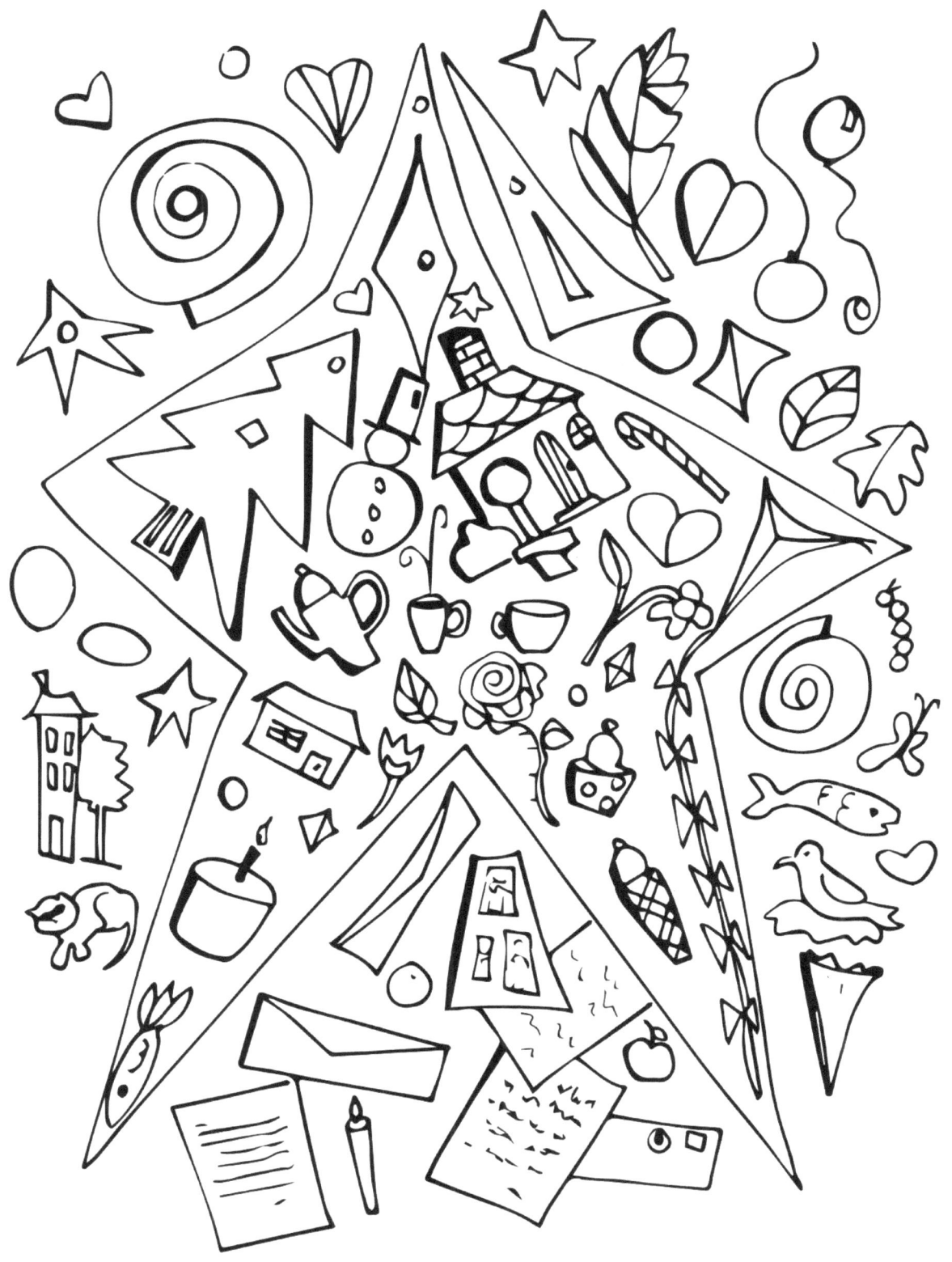

HERBS FILL THE SPACES
IN A GARDEN
AND IN A HEART.
COLOR THEM
SPLENDID.
LAVENDER, BASIL,
SAGE, DILL, AND
OREGANO!
COLOR THEM
AND MAKE THEM GROW!

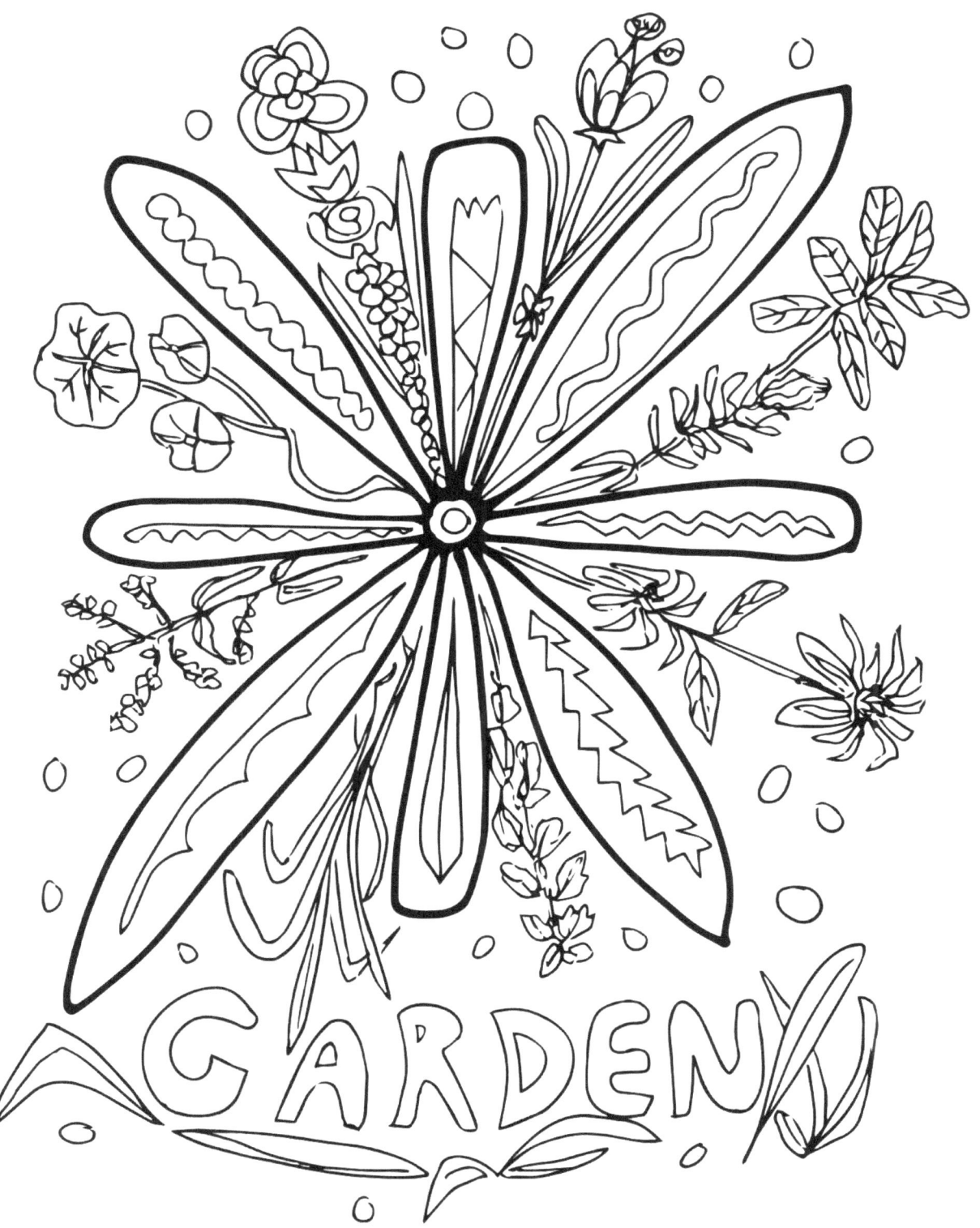

HOME AND HEARTS AND COFFEE CUPS

VIE FOR TIME AND COMPANY.

HOLD THEM CLOSE.

COLOR THEM WELL.

FOR TIME WILL TRY TO

EMPTY.

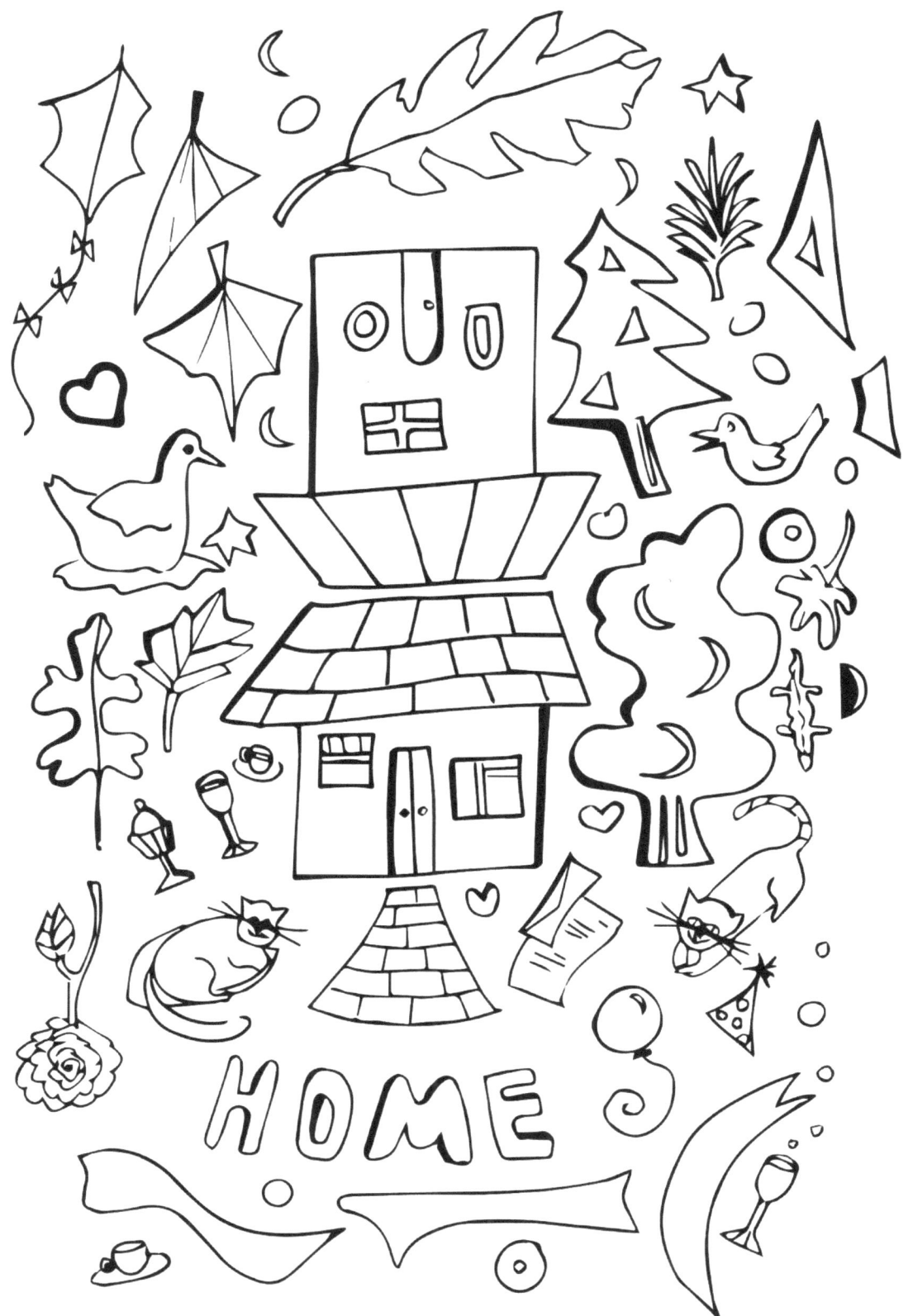

PINE TREE BEDECKED,

SCARLET GLASS BALLS,

SOFT FEATHERS, CRISP LEAVES,

CATS CURLED BY CHAIRS

IN CONES OF MOONLIGHT

PASSING THE STARTLED GOLD STARS.

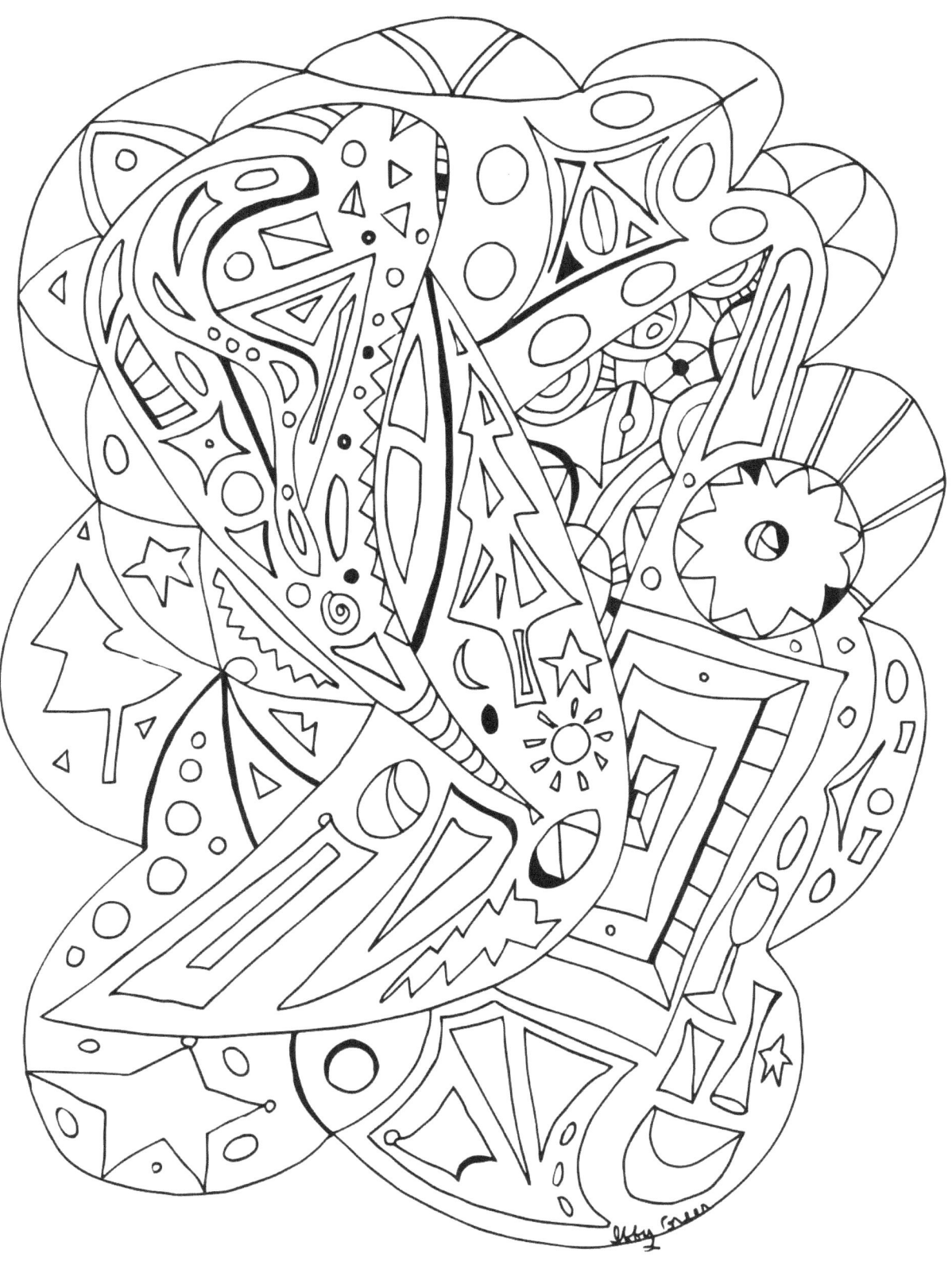

GARDEN BLOOMS TOPPLING AND TALL,

GROWING IN A PAPER GARDEN FOR ALL

TO WONDER AT GENUS, THE SPECIES,

THE NAME.

JUST COLOR THEM GLORIOUS,

COLOR THEM GRAND.

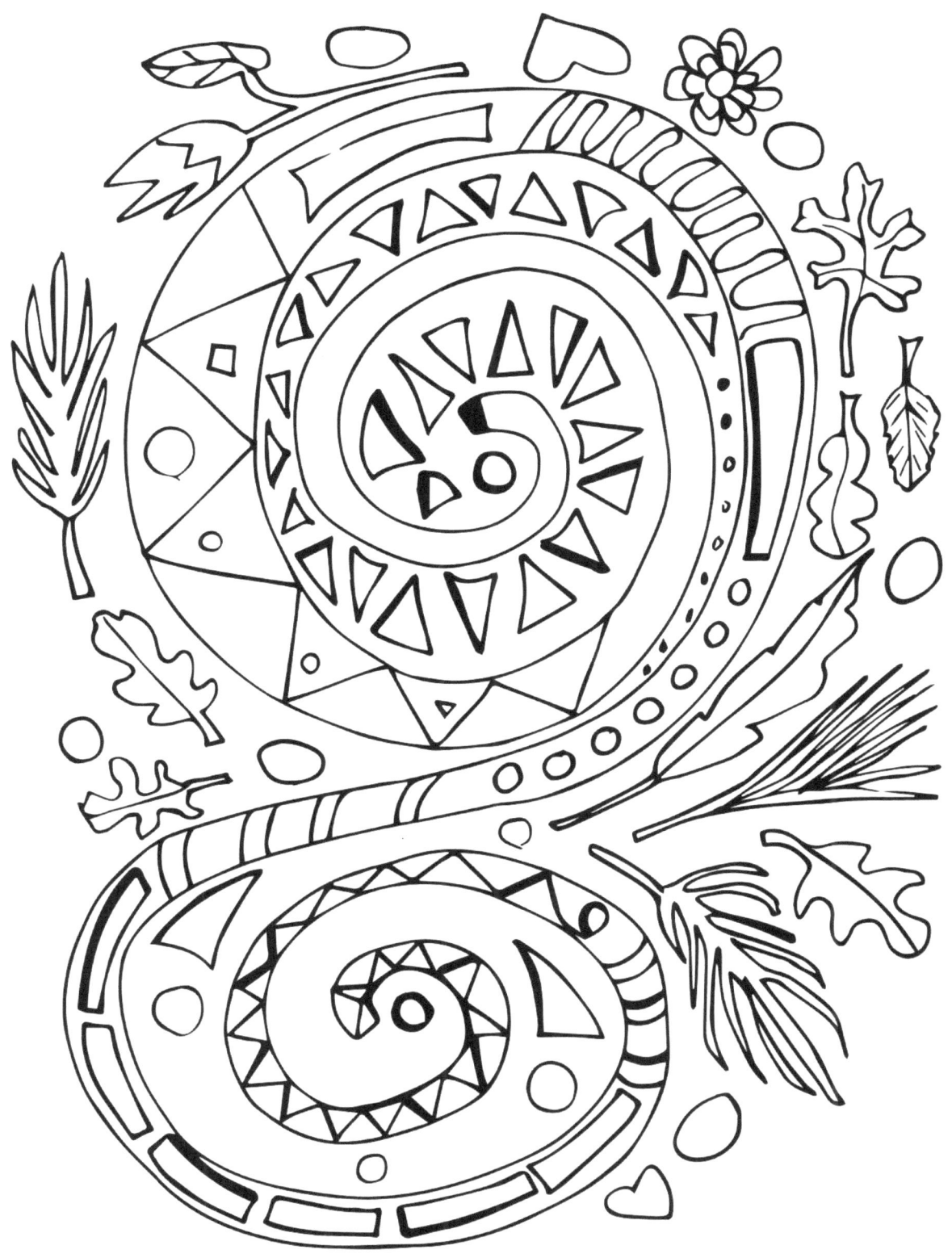

SOME SEE ANCIENT GODS IN THE NIGHT SKIES.
SOME SEE DIPPERS AND DOGS.
HOW ABOUT COLORING SOME CATS
OUT THERE AMONG THE FLEEING STARS?

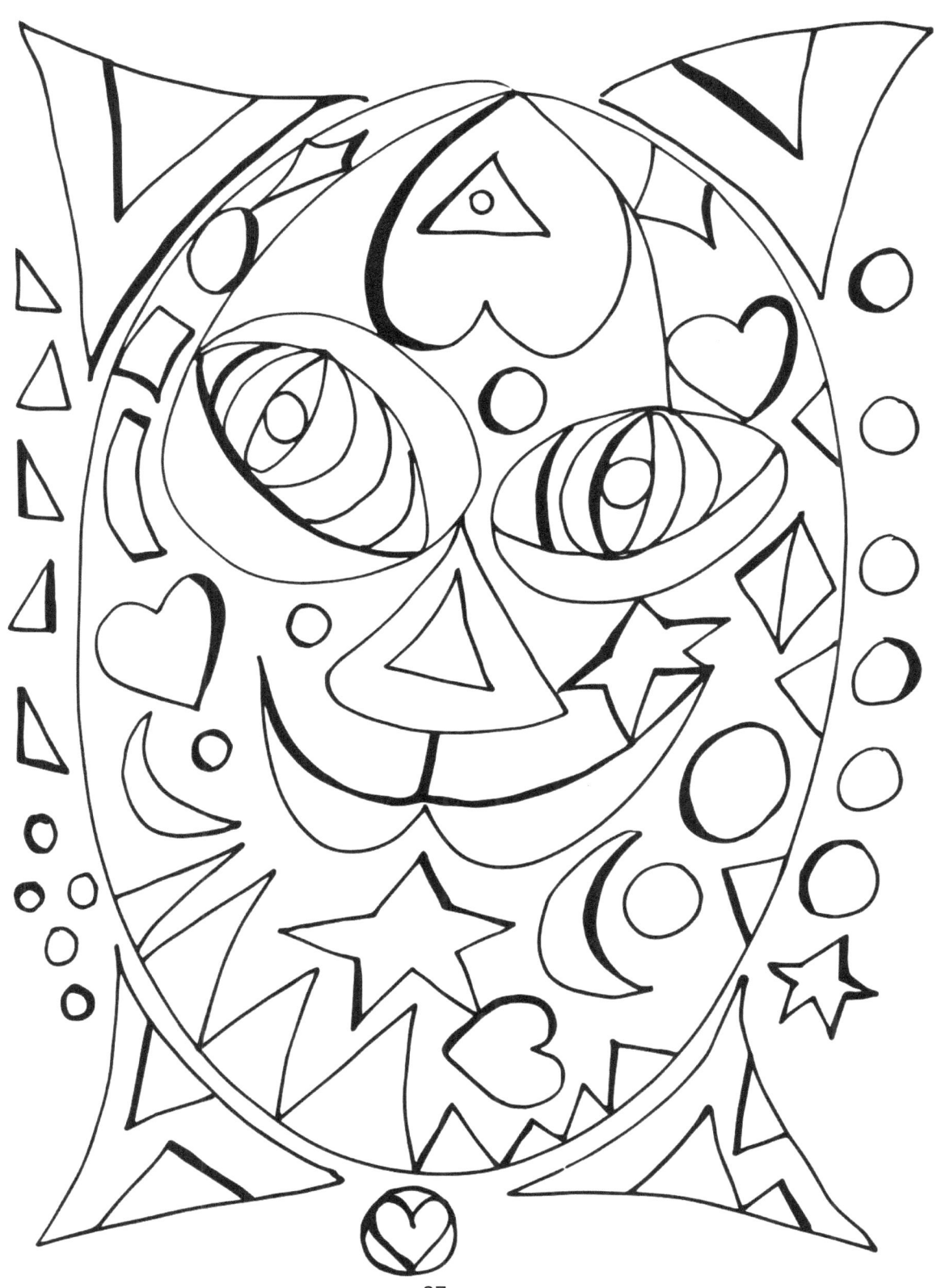

SHARP-SIDED TRIANGLE,

WHERE DO YOU LIVE?

SAME FOR YOU, SQUARE, DANCING IN AIR:

KEEPING COMPANY WITH A WANDERING STAR.

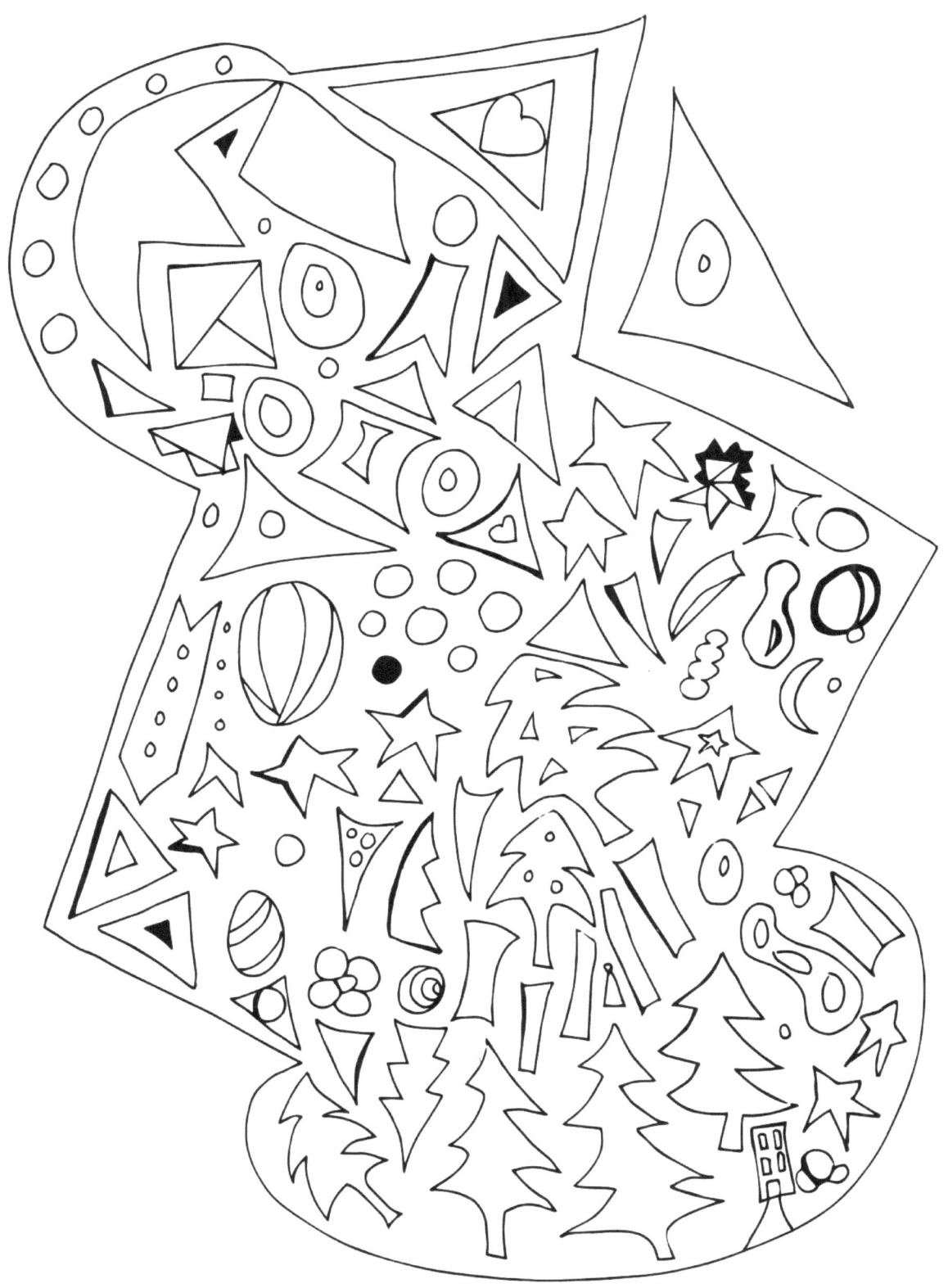

PENCIL OR CRAYON, WHATEVER THE HUE,

CRIMSON OR OCHRE, CINNABAR OR BLUE:

LEAVE YOUR RICH FLOURISHES HERE ON EACH SHAPE.

WITH EVERY COLOR CREATE A NEW SPACE.

EACH SCALLOP AND DOODLE

AWAITS A NEW LOOK.

YOUR COLORING BRINGS BEAUTY

AND PEACE TO THIS BOOK.

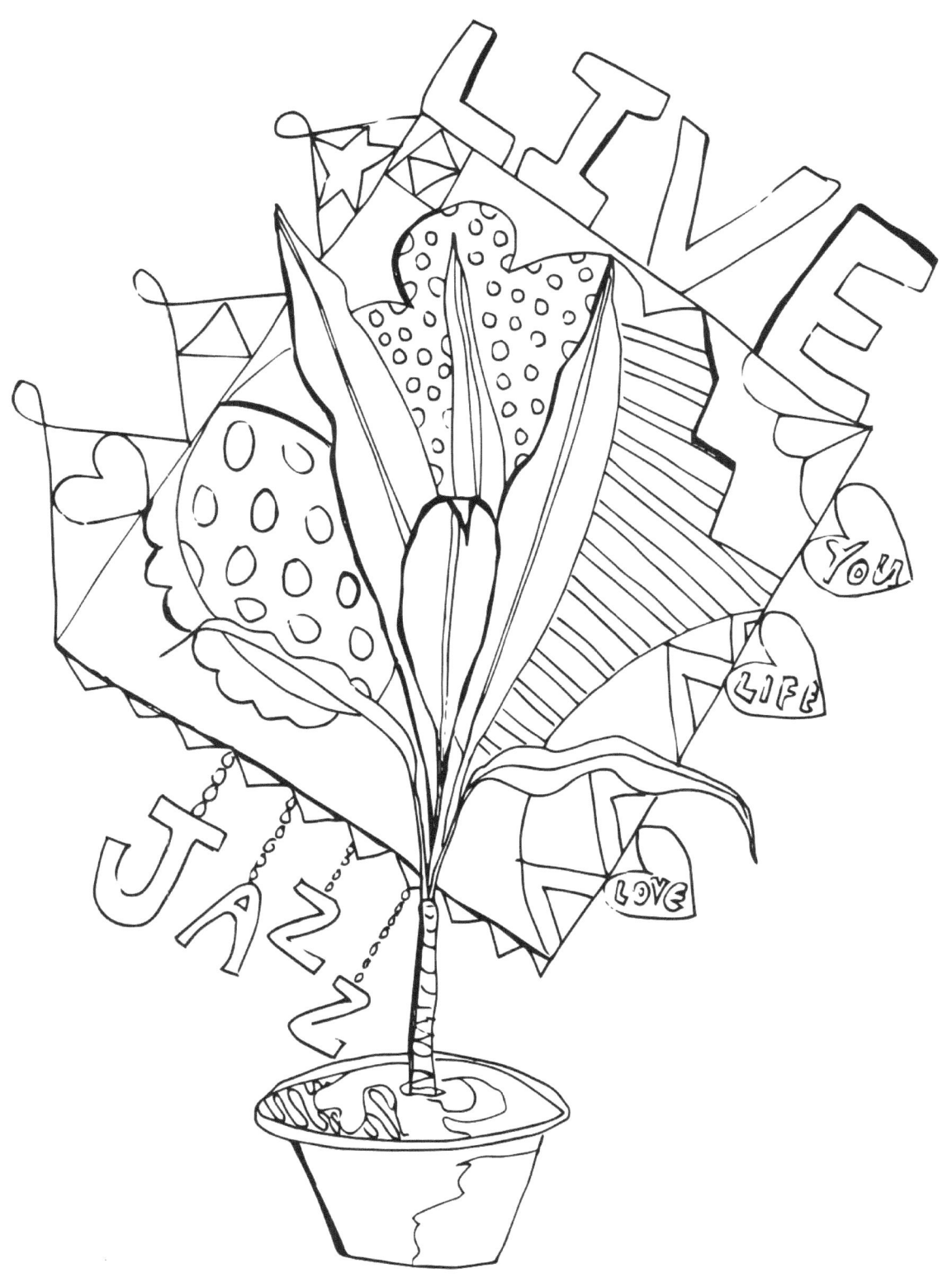

TRIANGLES BUMP AGAINST A STAR...

CIRCLES DRIFT AND SQUARES TUMBLE.

BIRDS AND FLOWERS SWIRL BEYOND

WHERE SHAPES AND CLOUDS RUMBLE.

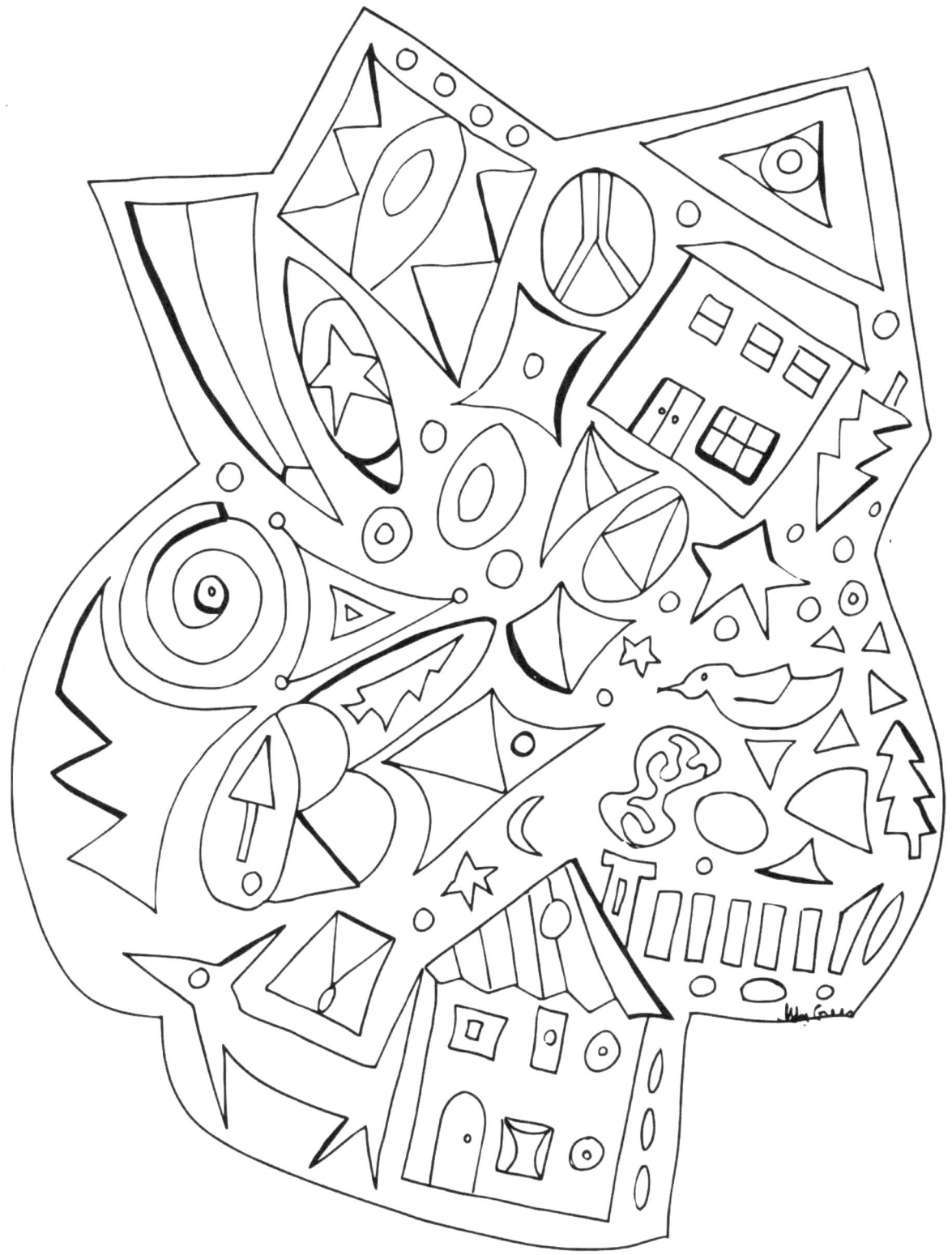

FEEL FREE TO WRITE AND SHARE YOUR FEELINGS AND
THOUGHTS AS YOU COLORED THIS BOOK.

etgreer@cox.net

P.O. BOX 4687
ROANOKE, VA 24015

USA

THE BOOK IS AVAILABLE ONLINE, AND DIRECTLY FROM
THE AUTHOR. SHIPPING AND HANDLING ADDED.

ABOUT THE AUTHOR

IBBY GREER, BORN IN THE MIDDLE OF THE LAST CENTURY,
STANDS ON THE PEAK OF THAT ERA AND LOOKS BACKWARDS
AND FORWARDS, HAPPY TO CONTRIBUTE TO A WORLD
WHERE EVERYONE COLORS.
COLORING IS COOL.

SEE HER WEBSITE, WWW.MOONSHINEWIDOW.COM FOR MORE
ABOUT HER OTHER BOOKS, OIL PAINTINGS,
AND HAND-PAINTED HARDSHELL GOURDS, "GOURDFRIENDS."

www.ingramcontent.com/pod-product-compliance
Lightning Source LLC
Chambersburg PA
CBHW050407180526
45159CB00005B/2179